Aquatic Invertebrate Monitoring at Tallgrass Prairie National Preserve, 2009 Status Report

Natural Resource Data Series NPS/HTLN/NRDS—2012/268

J. Tyler Cribbs and David E Bowles

National Park Service
Heartland I&M Network
6424 W Farm Road 182
Republic, MO 65738

March 2012

U.S. Department of the Interior
National Park Service
Natural Resource Stewardship and Science
Fort Collins, Colorado

The National Park Service, Natural Resource Stewardship and Science office in Fort Collins, Colorado publishes a range of reports that address natural resource topics of interest and applicability to a broad audience in the National Park Service and others in natural resource management, including scientists, conservation and environmental constituencies, and the public.

The Natural Resource Data Series is intended for the timely release of basic data sets and data summaries. Care has been taken to assure accuracy of raw data values, but a thorough analysis and interpretation of the data has not been completed. Consequently, the initial analyses of data in this report are provisional and subject to change.

All manuscripts in the series receive the appropriate level of peer review to ensure that the information is scientifically credible, technically accurate, appropriately written for the intended audience, and designed and published in a professional manner. This report received informal peer review by subject-matter experts who were not directly involved in the collection, analysis, or reporting of the data.

Views, statements, findings, conclusions, recommendations, and data in this report do not necessarily reflect views and policies of the National Park Service, U.S. Department of the Interior. Mention of trade names or commercial products does not constitute endorsement or recommendation for use by the U.S. Government.

This report is available from (http://science.nature.nps.gov/im/units/htln) and the Natural Resource Publications Management website (http://www.nature.nps.gov/publications/nrpm/).

Please cite this publication as:

Cribbs J. Tyler and D. E. Bowles. 2012. Aquatic invertebrate monitoring at Tallgrass Prairie National Preserve, 2009 status report. Natural Resource Data Series NPS/HTLN/NRDS—2012/268. National Park Service, Fort Collins, Colorado.

NPS 031/113317, March 2012

Contents

Tables

Abstract

Tallgrass Prairie National Preserve (TAPR) is the first National Park Service area established specifically for the preservation, protection, and interpretation of a tallgrass prairie ecosystem. The Heartland Inventory and Monitoring Network began monitoring water quality and invertebrate community structure of two streams (Palmer Creek and Fox Creek) within TAPR's boundary during September 2009. A Surber stream bottom sampler was used to collect 9 benthic samples from each stream. Habitat data were collected from the sampling net frame, and water quality data were recorded hourly using a data logger. This report summarizes baseline aquatic invertebrate monitoring data. Water quality met the Kansas aquatic life criteria for prairie streams. The aquatic invertebrate data provided mixed results, however. EPT richness was low for each stream suggesting impairment, but % EPT abundance, EPT ratio, and moderate tolerance indices (HBI) for both streams did not suggest impairment. Fox Creek and Palmer Creek had similar scores for invertebrate community indices, and several intolerant taxa were represented in samples from both creeks. The invertebrate metrics presented in this report are generally comparable to those observed for other regional streams. Thus, preliminary data offer mixed results and are currently insufficient to fully characterize the integrity of Fox and Palmer creeks.

Acknowledgments

We thank Jan Hinsey, Samantha Muller, Myranda Clark, and Kristen Hase for their assistance with this project. Lloyd Morrison and Sherry Middlemis-Brown provided constructive comments on an earlier version of this report.

Introduction

Tallgrass Prairie National Preserve (TAPR) is the first National Park Service area established specifically for the preservation, protection, and interpretation of a tallgrass prairie ecosystem (Hiebert 1998). A vast North American prairie once covered over 160 million hectares, but over 95% of this resource has been destroyed by human encroachment making it one of the most endangered biomes on the continent (Samson and Knopf 1994). Prairie streams formed critical parts of those Great Plains ecosystems, and as the prairie was lost, so were the streams (Dodds et al. 2004). Many of the remaining prairie fragments are not sufficiently large to support proper ecological functioning of their resident streams (Hall et al. 2003, Dodds et al. 2004). Today, prairie streams continue to face anthropogenic threats and understanding their ecology has become critically important (Dodds et al. 2004). Although some of the prairie streams and their watersheds at TAPR are largely protected, they remain vulnerable to human disturbance. Periodic monitoring of their biological communities will help detect disturbances and their associated impacts. Aquatic invertebrates are an important biological tool for understanding and detecting changes in stream ecosystem integrity, and they can be used to reflect cumulative impacts that cannot otherwise be detected through traditional water quality monitoring.

The Heartland Inventory and Monitoring Network (HTLN) began monitoring water quality and invertebrate community structure in Palmer and Fox creeks at TAPR in September 2009. The monitoring objectives of this study are: 1) determine the status and trends of invertebrate species diversity, abundance, and community metrics, and 2) relate the invertebrate community to overall water quality through quantification of metrics related to taxa richness, abundance, diversity, and region-specific multi-metric indices as indicators of water quality and habitat conditions. The purpose of this report is to summarize baseline aquatic invertebrate monitoring data collected during September 2009.

Methods

Methods and procedures used in this report follow Bowles *et al.* (2008), Monitoring Protocol for Aquatic Invertebrates of Small Streams in the Heartland Inventory & Monitoring Network. Samples were collected at one reach of Palmer Creek and one reach of Fox Creek (Figure 1). Three successive riffles were sampled with three benthic invertebrate samples collected at each riffle, resulting in nine total samples for each creek. A Surber stream bottom sampler (500 μm mesh, 0.09 m^2) was used to collect the samples. Samples were sorted in the laboratory following a subsampling routine described in Bowles et al. (2008). Taxa were identified to the lowest practical taxonomic level (usually genus) and counted.

Metrics calculated for each sample included genus richness, Shannon diversity index, EPT (Ephemeroptera, Plecoptera, Trichoptera) richness, EPT ratio (EPT density/(EPT density + Chironomidae density)), genus evenness (where 0 = minimum evenness, 1 = maximum evenness), % EPT abundance (i.e., the percentage of the total invertebrate abundance comprised of EPT), and Hilsenhoff biotic index (HBI). Shannon's index accounts for both abundance and evenness of the species present and index values are greater when all taxa in a sample are equally abundant. For biological data, values of Shannon's index typically range from 1.5 (low species richness and evenness) to 3.5 (high species evenness and richness). In comparison, evenness index values increase as the index approaches 1. The HBI is calculated using tolerance values (TV) assigned

1

to individual taxa. A TV between 0 and 3 would be classified as intolerant and values from 7 to 10 would be classified as tolerant (Barbour et al. 1999). By definition, HBI scores range from 0 to 10, with ten indicating the most disturbance. In addition to EPT richness, % EPT abundance is used to assess stream integrity in Kansas (USEPA 2005, Table 1) and was therefore included in this study. The biological criteria included in Table 1 are descriptors of the numerical benchmark values that describe the reference aquatic communities inhabiting waters that have been given a designated aquatic life use (Goodrich et al. 2005). The primary purpose of these biological criteria is to establish regional attainment goals that are relevant to aquatic life use and resource protection. The categories of biological criteria are biological supporting; partially biological supporting; and non-biological supporting. Higher metric values are associated with better stream conditions, except for HBI where smaller values indicate better conditions. We did not calculate the Macroinvertebrate Biotic Index (MBI) or the Kansas Biotic Index (KBI) used by the Kansas Department of Health and Environment, (KDHE) because these two indices are based on less sensitive family level identifications than the HBI we used, which uses genus level identifications. The KBI is analogous to the family level HBI (Huggins and Moffett 1988).

For each sample, current velocity (meters/second) and depth (cm) were recorded directly in front of the sampling net frame. Qualitative habitat variables (embeddedness, periphyton, filamentous algae, aquatic vegetation, deposition, and organic material) were estimated within the sampling net frame as percentage categories (0, <10, 10-40, 40-75, >75). Habitat category midpoint values were used in analysis calculations. Dominant substrate size from the area within the sampling net frame was visually assessed using the Wentworth scale (Wentworth 1922). Stream discharge was measured upstream of the sampled riffles. Water quality readings were recorded hourly using a calibrated YSI 6920 or YSI 6600 data logger. The water quality and habitat data presented in this report represent only a snapshot of the broad temporal range of conditions and should be cautiously interpreted. They are intended to describe the prevailing conditions that influence the structure of invertebrate communities, and they may help explain variability between samples, but they should not be used as an analytical tool in the strictest sense (Bowles et al. 2008). Due to the limitations of using water quality data obtained with data loggers, the invertebrate community is used here as a surrogate of the long-term water quality condition of Palmer and Fox creeks. Water quality criteria for Kansas streams are shown in Table 2.

Park Boundary
Streams
○ Fox Sample Si
● Palmer Sample

Figure 1. Location of sampling sites on Palmer Creek and Fox Creek, Tallgrass Prairie National Preserve.

Table 1. Biological supporting criteria for EPT richness and percent EPT abundance (USEPA 2005).

Supporting Criteria	EPT Richness	% EPT Abundance
Fully supporting	≥13	≥48
Partially supporting	8-12	31-47
Non-supporting	≤8	≤30

Table 2. Kansas Aquatic Life Criteria (KDHE 2004).

Dissolved Oxygen (DO)	pH	Temperature (°C)
Shall not fall below 5.0	6.5-8.5	Shall not exceed 32.0

Results

Fox Creek

A total of 41 taxa were collected in Fox Creek in 2009; 39% of which were EPT. (Appendix A). Mean genus richness across riffles was 16.89 (range= 14-21) (Table 3). Roughly one-fourth of all taxa collected were sensitive, having TVs of 3 or less. Sensitive taxa present in samples included the caddisfly (Trichoptera) genera *Chimarra* (TV= 2.8, 18.8% of the total benthic sample) and the riffle beetle *Microcylloepus* (Coleoptera) (TV= 2.1). The HBI values were moderate among riffles with scores ranging from 4.7-6.0 (mean= 5.3). Mean EPT richness for Fox Creek was 8 indicating this stream is partially supporting of biological life under the KDHE criteria. Conversely, mean % EPT abundance for Fox Creek (67.6%) indicates this stream is fully supporting of biological life. EPT taxa were dominant among samples, comprising 72.6% of total individuals, and the most prevalent taxon was the tolerant caddisfly (Trichoptera) genus *Cheumatopsyche* (TV= 6.6), making up 26% of the benthic density. The relatively high EPT ratio for Fox Creek (0.77) indicates that the dipteran family Chironomidae did not dominate a substantial portion of the benthic community among samples. The percentage composition of Chironomidae in the total benthic community varied greatly from 1.5% to 57.8% (mean= 14.8%). Shannon's index among samples ranged from 1.69 to 2.39 (mean= 2.0). Genus evenness ranged from 0.57 to 0.81 (mean= 0.69). Metric data for all samples and collection sites are shown in Appendix A.

Table 3. Summary statistics for invertebrate samples collected for Fox Creek, Tallgrass Prairie National Preserve, in 2009.

Statistic	Mean	Standard Error	Minimum	Maximum	N
Family Richness	15.44	0.90	11	19	9
Genus Richness	16.89	0.90	14	21	9
Shannon's Index	2.00	0.08	1.69	2.39	9
EPT Richness	8.00	0.05	6	11	9
EPT Ratio	0.77	0.09	0.31	0.98	9
% EPT Abundance	67.65	8.22	25.69	90.15	9
Genus Evenness	0.69	0.03	0.57	0.81	9
HBI	5.26	0.16	4.72	6.01	9

Water quality data for Fox Creek are summarized in Table 4. The mean water temperature reported for Fox Creek was 20.0°C. Mean dissolved oxygen level was 8.7 (range= 7.02-11.13). Specific conductance was at an acceptable level for the region (486.7 µS/cm), as was mean pH (7.83). Stream discharge was 0.02 m³/s at the time of invertebrate sampling.

Table 4. Water quality data for Fox Creek, Tallgrass Prairie National Preserve. Data were collected hourly with calibrated data loggers from September 2-9, 2009.

Water Quality Statistic	Mean	Standard Deviation	Minimum	Maximum	N
Temperature (°C)	20.00	1.02	17.89	22.48	182
Specific Conductance (µS/cm)	486.71	7.68	473.00	500.00	182
Dissolved Oxygen (mg/liter)	8.71	1.07	7.02	11.13	182
pH	7.83	0.06	7.72	7.97	182
Turbidity (NTU)	4.83	1.32	2.90	8.70	182

Habitat among riffles was uniform (Table 5). Riffles were very shallow (mean= 7.6 cm) with moderate current velocity (mean= 0.38 m/sec). Mean substrate size values at all three riffles were nearly a 14 on the Wentworth scale, (range= 10-16; 10-83 mm, small pebble to cobble). Embeddedness and deposition were moderate (means= 32.2% and 53.6%, respectively). Percentage of periphyton in samples was 35.8% among samples, and no aquatic vegetation was present. Percentage of organic material in samples was moderate at 24.2%.

Table 5. Summary statistics for habitat variables associated with benthic samples collected from Fox Creek, Tallgrass Prairie National Preserve, in 2009.

Habitat Parameter	Mean	Standard Error	Minimum	Maximum	N
Depth (cm)	7.56	0.50	5	9	9
Current velocity (m/sec)	0.38	0.08	0.08	0.71	9
Substrate (Wentworth Scale)	13.89	0.65	10	16	9
Embeddedness (%)	32.22	4.78	25	57.5	9
Vegetation (%)	0	0	0	0	9
Filamentous algae (%)	47.22	8.63	0	87.5	9
Periphyton (%)	35.83	5.42	25	57.5	9
Deposition (%)	53.61	6.32	25	87.5	9
Organics (%)	24.17	5.07	5	57.5	9

Palmer Creek

A total of 36 taxa were collected during our 2009 sampling of Palmer Creek. Mean genus richness across riffles was 15.2 (range= 9-19) (Table 6). Mean EPT richness was relatively low (6.1), which would be classified as non-supporting under KDHE criteria. Similar to Fox Creek, the Palmer Creek mean % EPT abundance of nearly 52% meets the fully supporting biological criteria established by KDHE. The EPT ratio was 73% and the percentage composition of Chironomidae in the total benthic community ranged from 0%-49% (mean= 20%). In most samples, the three dominant taxa included Baetidae (TV= 4.0), Chironomidae (TV= 6.0), and the mayfly genus *Baetis* (TV= 6.0). Shannon's index among samples ranged from 1.76 to 2.23 (mean= 2.04). Genus evenness ranged from 0.67 to 0.86 (mean= 0.74). Sensitive taxa that were found include *Helicopsyche* (Trichoptera: Helicopsychidae), *Chimarra* (Trichoptera: Philopotamidae) and *Prosimulium* (Diptera: Simuliidae); all had TVs less than 3. The top three dominant taxa comprised the majority of benthic densities for all samples (range 8.8 to 21.3%, mean= 14.7%). HBI was moderate for all samples ranging from 4.36 to 5.84 (mean= 5.20). Metric data for all samples and collection sites are shown in Appendix A.

Table 6. Summary statistics for invertebrate samples collected for Palmer Creek, Tallgrass Prairie National Preserve, in 2009.

Statistic	Mean	Standard Error	Minimum	Maximum	N
Family Richness	14.56	1.08	8	18	9
Genus Richness	15.22	1.09	9	19	9
Shannon's Index	2.04	0.05	1.76	2.23	9
EPT Richness	6.10	0.42	5	8	9
EPT Ratio	0.73	0.07	0.37	1.00	9
% EPT Abundance	51.77	4.49	28.30	71.79	9
Genus Evenness	0.74	0.02	0.67	0.86	9
HBI	5.20	0.17	4.36	5.84	9

Water quality data for Palmer Creek are summarized in Table 7. The mean water temperature reported for Palmer Creek was 18.4°C. Mean dissolved oxygen levels were 8.0 (range= 5.6-11.0). Specific conductance was at an acceptable level for the region (587.5 µS/cm), as was mean pH (7.6). Stream discharge was 0.0005 m^3/s at the time of invertebrate sampling.

Table 7. Water quality data for Palmer Creek, Tallgrass Prairie National Preserve. Data were collected hourly with calibrated data loggers from September 2-10, 2009.

Water Quality Statistic	Mean	Standard Deviation	Minimum	Maximum	N
Temperature ($^{\circ}$C)	18.4	0.74	16.5	19.6	188
Specific Conductance (µS/cm)	587.54	20.7	488.0	610.0	188
Dissolved Oxygen (mg/liter)	8.0	1.4	5.6	11.0	188
pH	7.6	0.1	7.3	7.9	188
Turbidity (NTU)	1.96	4.8	0	54.8	188

Habitat among riffles was uniform (Table 8). Riffles were very shallow (mean= 3.2 cm) with relatively slow current velocity (mean= 0.12 m/sec). Mean substrate at all three riffles was nearly a 15 on the Wentworth scale (range= 12-17; 22.1-117 mm, small pebble to cobble). Embeddedness and deposition were moderate (means= 35.8% and 50%, respectively). Percentage of periphyton in substrate was 54% among samples, and no aquatic vegetation was present in samples. Percentage of organic material in samples was moderate at 23%.

Table 8. Summary statistics for habitat variables associated with benthic samples collected from Palmer Creek, Tallgrass Prairie National Preserve, in 2009.

Habitat Parameter	Mean	Standard Error	Minimum	Maximum	N
Depth (cm)	3.22	0.28	2	4	9
Current velocity (m/sec)	0.12	0.02	0.02	0.23	9
Substrate (Wentworth Scale)	14.78	0.52	12	17	9
Embeddedness (%)	35.83	5.42	25	57.5	9
Vegetation (%)	0	0	0	0	9
Filamentous algae (%)	0.56	0.56	0	5	9
Periphyton (%)	53.89	3.61	25	57.5	9
Deposition (%)	50.28	4.78	25	57.5	9
Organics (%)	22.78	2.22	5	25	9

Discussion

A previous survey of Fox Creek conducted by the United States Environmental Protection Agency (USEPA 2008) indicated this stream did not meet aquatic life criteria because it only partially supported biological communities. This judgment was based on assessments of aquatic invertebrate, fecal coliform bacteria, suspended solids and sulfates that did not compare favorably with those of regional reference streams. Similarly, Palmer Creek was listed as partially supporting based upon invertebrate samples (USEPA 2005). Water quality collected in this study met the Kansas aquatic life criteria (KDHE 2004) for prairie streams. The aquatic invertebrate data presented in this study provided mixed results. EPT richness was low for each stream suggesting impairment, but % EPT abundance, EPT ratio, and moderate tolerance indices (HBI) for both streams do not indicate impairment, which suggest these streams are functioning normally. Fox Creek and Palmer Creek both had similar scores for invertebrate community indices. Several intolerant taxa were represented in samples from Fox Creek (21% of the total individuals) and Palmer Creek (8.3%). The invertebrate metrics presented in this report are generally comparable to those observed for other regional streams, and suggest the data for Fox and Palmer creeks fall within a normal range for the region (MacFarlane 1983, Harris et al. 1991, 1999, Bass 1994, Whiles et al. 2000, Hall et al. 2003, Sarver et al. 2002, Zelt and Frankforter 2003, Kosnicki and Sites 2007, Poulton et al. 2007, Hutchens et al. 2009).

Collectively, these inconclusive data suggest that Fox Creek and Palmer Creek may be mildly impaired, although such a designation is not decisive. Both Fox Creek and Palmer Creek have occasionally been reported to have elevated nitrogen and phosphorus levels that potentially can cause biological degradation (USEPA 2005, 2008). The majority of the Palmer Creek watershed within TAPR is characterized as prairie, and it is subject to minimal anthropogenic disturbance. In comparison, numerous anthropogenic stressors occur in Fox Creek's watershed upstream of TAPR (USEPA 2005, 2008). The intermittent nature of prairie streams, including those in this study, may also serve as seasonal stressors, which could cause them to appear impaired (Lytle 2002). Continued monitoring of invertebrate communities will provide important water quality information to TAPR resource managers regarding the health of Fox Creek and Palmer Creek's respective watersheds.

Literature Cited

Barbour, M. T., J. Gerritsen, B. D. Snyder, and J. B. Stribling. 1999. Rapid bioassessment protocols for use in streams and wadeable rivers: Periphyton, benthic macroinvertebrate, and fish, 2nd ed. EPA 841-B-99-002, U.S. Environmental Protection Agency, Washington, DC.

Bass, D. 1994. Community Structure and Distribution Patterns of Aquatic Macroinvertebrates in a Tall Grass Prairie Stream Ecosystem Proceedings Oklahoma Academy Science **74**:3-10.

Bowles, D.E., M.H. Williams, H. R. Dodd, L. W. Morrison, J.A. Hinsey, C.E. Ciak, G.A. Rowell, M. D. DeBacker, and J. L. Haack. 2008. Monitoring Protocol for Aquatic Invertebrates of Small Streams in the Heartland Inventory & Monitoring Network. Natural Resource Report NPS/HTLN/NRR 2008/042. National Park Service, Fort Collins, Colorado.

Dodds, W. K., K. Gido, M. R. Whiles, K. M. Fritz, and W. J. Matthews. 2004. Life on the Edge: The Ecology of Great Plains Prairie Streams. BioScience **54**:205-216.

Goodrich, C., D. G. Huggins, R. C. Everhart, E. F. Smith. 2005. Summary of State and National Biological and Physical Habitat Assessment Methods with a Focus on US EPA Region 7 States Report No. 135 of the Kansas Biological Survey, Lawrence, Kansas.

Hall, D. L., B. S. Bergthold, and R. W. Sites. 2003. The influence of adjacent land use on macroinvertebrate communities of prairie streams in Missouri. Journal of Freshwater Ecology **18**:55-68.

Harris, M. A., B. C. Kondratieff, and T. P. Boyle. 1991. Invertebrate assemblages and water quality in six National Park units in the Great Plains. National Park Service, Water Resources Division, Fort Collins, Colorado.

Harris, M. A., B. C. Kondratieff, and T. P. Boyle. 1999. Macroinvertebrate community structure of three prairie streams. Journal of the Kansas Entomological Society **72**:402-425.

Hiebert, R.D. 1998. Opportunities to enhance and maintain the tallgrass prairie ecosystem with the boundaries of Tallgrass Prairie National Preserve. United States Department of Interior, United States National Park Service, unpublished report.

Huggins, D. G., and M. Moffett. 1988. Proposed biotic and habitat indices for use in Kansas Streams. Report No. 35 of the Kansas Biological Survey. University of Kansas, Lawrence, Kansas. Second printing (electronic reformatting), November 2003.

Hutchens, J. J., Jr., J. A. Schuldt, C. Richards, L. B. Johnson, G. E. Host, and D. H. Breneman. 2009. Multi-scale mechanistic indicators of Midwestern USA stream macroinvertebrates. Ecological Indicators **9**:1138–1150

Kansas Department of Health and Environment (KDHE). 2004. Kansas surface water quality standards, table of numeric criteria. Topeka, Kansas.

Kosnicki, E., and R. W. Sites. 2007. Least-desired index for assessing the effectiveness of grass riparian filter strips in improving water quality in an agricultural region. Environmental Entomology **36**:713-724.

Lytle, D.A. 2002. Flash floods and aquatic insect life-history evolution: Evaluation of multiple models. Ecology **83**:370–385.

MacFarlane, M. B. 1983. Structure of benthic macroinvertebrate communities in a Midwestern plains stream. Freshwater Invertebrate Biology **2**:147-153.

Poulton, B. C., T. J. Rasmussen, and C. J. Lee. 2007. Assessment of biological conditions at selected stream sites in Johnson County, and Cass County and Jackson counties, Missouri, 2003 and 2004. U.S. Geological Survey Special Investigations Report 2007-5108.

Samson, F., and F. Knopf. 1994. Prairie conservation in North America.BioScience **44**:418–421.

Sarver, R., S. Harlan, C. Rabeni, and S. Sowa. 2002. Biological Criteria for Wadeable/Perennial Streams of Missouri. Missouri Department of Natural Resources, Jefferson City, Missouri.

United States Environmental Protection Agency (USEPA). 2005. Neosho River Basin total maximum daily load, water body: Fox Creek Watershed including Palmer Creek Water Quality Impairment: Biology (http://www.epa.gov/region7/water/pdf/foxcreek_watershd_bio_final_010605.pdf). Accessed January 3, 2012

United States Environmental Protection Agency (USEPA). 2008. 2008 Water Quality Assessment and TMDL Information. (http://iaspub.epa.gov/waters10/attains_waterbody.control?p_au_id=KS1107020319). Accessed August 15, 2011

Whiles, M. R., B. L. Brock, A. C. Franzen, and S. C. Dinsmore, II. 2000. Stream Invertebrate Communities, Water Quality, and Land-Use Patterns in an Agricultural Drainage Basin of Northeastern Nebraska, USA. Environmental Management **26**:563-576.

Wentworth, C. K. 1922. A scale of grade and class terms for clastic sediments. Journal of Geology **30**:377-392.

Zelt, R. B., and J. D. Frankforter. 2003. Water-quality assessment of the central Nebraska basins—entering a new decade. USGS Fact Sheet 013–03. US Geological Survey, Lincoln, Nebraska.

Appendix. Aquatic invertebrate data collected from Tallgrass Prairie National Preserve (TAPR), in 2009.

Table A-1. Aquatic invertebrate data collected from Fox Creek, TAPR, 2009. TV is tolerance value. Riffles sampled are numerically designated as 1-3 and L, M and R refer to left, middle and right samples taken in a riffle.

Phylum	Class	Order	Family	Genus	Tolerance Value	1 L	1 M	1 R	2 L	2 M	2 R	3 L	3 M	3 R
Annelida	Oligochaeta				8					4	8			
Arthropoda	Arachnoida	Hydracarina			5.7			8	40	20	8		4	32
		Bassommatophora	Planorbidae		7						4			
	Insecta	Coleoptera	Elmidae	Stenelmis	5.4	48	16	20	24	60	20	2	16	60
			Elmidae	Microcylloepus	2.1	20	28	14	16		4	8	52	24
			Hydrophilidae		5			2	4					
		Diptera	unknown		—									
			Ceratopogonidae	Bezzia	6		4		4	8		2		4
			Chironomidae		6	64	80	56	368	504	324	8	44	136
			Empididae	Hemerodromia	6			2	4					4
			Simuliidae	Simulium	4.4		16	4						
			Simuliidae	Prosimulium	2.6	12								
			Tabanidae	Tabanus	9.7			8	12		4	4	4	12
			Tipulidae	Hexatoma	4.7	16		8		8	24	6		12
			Tipulidae		3								4	
		Ephemeroptera	unknown		—		4		20	16	8			

Phylum	Class	Order	Family	Genus	Tolerance Value	1 L	1 M	1 R	2 L	2 M	2 R	3 L	3 M	3 R
			Baetidae		4	116	172	134	92	16	52	88	140	416
		Ephemeroptera	Baetidae	*Baetis*	6	408	96	52	40			24	28	56
			Caenidae	*Caenis*	7.6				8	36	20			
			Heptageniidae		4			2					4	
			Heptageniidae	*Stenacron*	7.1		36			8	4	2	12	
			Heptageniidae	*Stenonema*	3.4	8				4	4			8
			Isonychiidae	*Isonychia*	3.7	32	16	2				4		
			Leptophlebiidae	*Leptophlebia*	6.4		12			4	20	12	8	20
			Tricorythidae	*Tricorythodes*	5.4		8	6	84	96	60			8
		Limnophila	Ancylidae	*Ferrissia*	6.9			2						
		Limnophila	Physidae	*Physella*	9.1		4							
		Megaloptera	Corydalidae	*Corydalus*	5.6	44	24	22		8	20	12	16	24
		Megaloptera	Corydalidae	*Nigronia*	5.8	24		4						
		Odonata	Coenagrionidae	*Argia*	8.7			20		36	40		4	
		Plecoptera	unknown		2						4			
			Perlidae		1									
			Helicopsychidae	*Helicopsyche*	0	8			8		4			4
		Trichoptera	Hydropsychidae	*Ceratopsyche*	1.4	8	8							

14

Appendix A. Continued

Phylum	Class	Order	Family	Genus	Tolerance Value	1 L	1 M	1 R	2 L	2 M	2 R	3 L	3 M	3 R
			Hydropsychidae	Cheumatopsyche	6.6	388	132	128	92	16	64	178	296	1300
			Hydroptilidae	Hydroptila	6.2	24	60	12	40	20	8			8
			Hydroptilidae		4		4					8	32	
			Philopotamidae	Chimarra	2.8	384	104	150	60	8	4	160	264	652
		Tricladida	Planariidae	Dugesia	7.5			8				10	8	108
		Veneroidea	Corbiculidae	Corbicula	6.3				16					
Mollusca	Gastropoda	Limnophila	Physidae	Physella	9.1		4							

15

Table A-2. Aquatic invertebrate data collected from Palmer Creek, TAPR, 2009. TV=tolerance value. TV is tolerance value. Riffles sampled are numerically designated as 1-3 and L, M and R refer to left, middle and right samples taken in a riffle.

Phylum	Class	Order	Family	Genus	Tolerance Value	1 L	1 M	1 R	2 L	2 M	2 R	3 L	3 M	3 R
Annelida	Oligochaeta				8						1			
Arthropoda	Arachnoida	Hydracarina			5.7	2	2	2		1	1	6	8	3
		Bassommatophora	Planorbidae		7	2								
	Crustacea	Decapoda	Cambaridae	Orconectes	2.7	4								
	Insecta	Coleoptera	Elmidae	Stenelmis	5.4	110	74	5	1	2			6	
			Ceratopogonidae	Bezzia	6	2	2		1					1
			Ceratopogonidae	Forcipomyia	6								2	1
			Chironomidae		6	36	40		12	50	26	56	126	45
			Empididae	Hemerodromia	6				17	5	1	2	20	4
			Simuliidae		6					6		6		1
			Simuliidae	Prosimulium	2.6		24	1			4		2	
			Tabanidae	Tabanus	9.7	2	2	1		3	1	8	4	12
			Tipulidae	Hexatoma	4.7	6	10		1	2	2	2	6	7
			Tipulidae	Tipula	7.7						1			
		Ephemeroptera	Baetidae		4	34	32	7	31	31	3	118	84	91
			Baetidae	Baetis	6	62	104			9		12	2	27
			Heptageniidae		4	2		1	1	2				7
			Heptageniidae	Stenacron	7.1		2	1		2				3

16

Appendix B. Continued.

Phylum	Class	Order	Family	Genus	Tolerance Value	1 L	1 M	1 R	2 L	2 M	2 R	3 L	3 M	3 R
			Heptageniidae	Stenonema	3.4	2		1	1	2	8		4	3
			Tricorythidae	Tricorythodes	5.4					1				
		Megaloptera	Corydalidae	Corydalus	5.6	2	2		1	2		4		3
		Megaloptera	Sialidae	Sialis	7.5									1
		Odonata	unknown		--		4		2					
		Odonata	Coenagrionidae		9					6	1	4	34	15
		Plecoptera	unknown		2	2								
		Trichoptera	Helicopsychidae	Helicopsyche	0	110		1		2	1	4	12	8
			Hydropsychidae	Ceratopsyche	1.4						1			
			Hydropsychidae	Cheumatopsyche	6.6	12	28	4	7	2	1	80	36	28
			Hydroptilidae	Hydroptila	6.2		14					6	20	4
			Hydroptilidae		4	2			4	1				
			Philopotamidae		3				4	2				
			Philopotamidae	Chimarra	2.8	4	26				1	4	8	3
			Polycentropodidae	Polycentropus	3.5	4								
		Tricladida	Planariidae	Dugesia	7.5	72	42		3	5			2	1
		Veneroidea	Corbiculidae	Corbicula	6.3	4								
Mollusca	Gastropoda	Limnophila	Physidae	Physella	9.1									

www.ingramcontent.com/pod-product-compliance
Lightning Source LLC
Chambersburg PA
CBHW081153290526
45795CB00008B/2910